GW00372970

GARDENING F
FLOWER ARRANGER

RUTH LEDDER

HarperCollins*Publishers*

Products mentioned in this book

Benlate* + 'Activex' 2	contains	benomyl
'Rapid'	contains	pirimicarb
'Sybol' Dust	contains	pirimiphos-methyl

*Benlate is a registered trade mark of Du Pont's

Read the label before you buy; use insecticides safely

Editors Diana Brinton, Joey Chapter
Designer Gordon Robertson
Picture research Janet Grillet
Production Craig Chubb

First published in 1991 by
Harper Collins Publishers
London

© Marshall Cavendish Limited 1991

**A CIP catalogue record for this book
is available from the British Library.**

ISBN 0-00-412600-9

Photoset by Litho Link Ltd, Welshpool, Powys, Wales
Printed and bound in Hong Kong by Dai Nippon Printing Company

Front cover: Detail of a summer flower arrangement
Back cover: Nigella damascena 'Persian Jewels'
Both by the Hary Smith Horticultural Collection

CONTENTS

INTRODUCTION

The same elements and principles of design apply to flower arranging and to garden design as to any other art. In both cases, consideration must be given to colour, space, texture and form, all of which must be combined to create a harmonious whole. The aim of this book is to show how easy it is to create a garden that is pleasing to the eye and offers—all year round—a host of flowers and foliages for equally-pleasing arrangements in the home.

A brief history Flowers and plants have been used for pleasurable as well as practical purposes throughout history. The Greeks and Romans used flowers in ritual offerings to their gods. In India and China, Hindu and Buddhist priests used flowers in their offerings centuries before the birth of Christ.

In medieval times, people believed that plagues and infections were transmitted through ill-smelling airs, so they carried posies of sweet-scented herbs and flowers in order to ward off disease.

The Italian Renaissance period saw more use being made of cut flowers, while in Tudor England flowers were cut and arranged in the home for weddings, funerals and other occasions. Many of the flowers, such as pinks (gillyflowers), that were cultivated in 16th-century gardens are grown in our gardens and arranged in our homes today.

In the 17th century, a period of considerable Dutch and Flemish influence, an increasing range of flowers was used in lavish designs in vases and urns. This era saw the birth of 'Tulipmania', with fortunes being made and lost in the hunt for new tulip cultivars. Plantsmen such as the Tradescants, father and son, searched the Old World and the New for exotic species. The hunt for new plants continued, and towards the end of the century Queen Mary herself commissioned collectors to bring back exotics.

The vast range of interesting new plants could not successfully be grown in a traditional parterre without spoiling its symmetry, so it became necessary to set aside separate areas. At the same time, the passion for evergreen plants, or 'greens', that could be grown in tubs and kept indoors in the winter led to the development of the greenhouse.

During the 18th and early 19th centuries, the arts of gardening and flower arranging continued to develop separately. Lancelot 'Capability' Brown developed the English landscaped park, creating many gar-

Alliums, achilleas, lychnis and lilies are all ideal for the arranger.

Annuals in the RHS's Wisley gardens.

the public during Queen Victoria's reign, and in 1804 the London Horticultural Society was formed, which later became the Royal Horticultural Society. Now, the Society's gardens at Wisley cover approximately 240 acres. Victorian gardeners used colourful plants for bedding out schemes, the brightest of them all being the annuals.

Gertrude Jekyll, who was born in 1843 and whose garden at Munstead won her praise and world renown, knew the value of combining appropriate plants to create a garden that would not only give material for decorating the home, but would be harmonious in its texture, colour and form.

dens that remain tourist attractions to this day. At the same time, large houses made great use of floral decorations, with either fresh or dried material. Table designs were large and ornate, and flowers were grown in the kitchen garden to supply the demand.

The Victorian era The Victorians were great lovers of plants and gardens, and it was during this period that flowers found their way back into the main garden and the two art forms—gardening and flower arranging—began to be seen as complementary. Flowers were used everywhere and anywhere. Clusters of plants would decorate empty fireplaces in the summer months; flowers were worn in the hair, carried in posies and worn as corsages. Churches were decorated with huge displays of foliage, flowers and pot plants. Dining tables groaned under the weight of epergnes filled with glorious arrangements of flowers.

Kew Gardens was first opened to

The 20th century Jekyll's work continued well into this century— *Colour in the Flower Garden* was published in 1908—and she influenced many others, including Vita Sackville-West, with her natural and at the same time artistic approach to garden design. In the 1930s Constance Spry achieved a similar revolution in flower arrangement, introducing an easy and relaxed style that used both wild and garden plant material.

During World War 2 most gardens were used to produce food to help feed the people, but some flowers were still available to brighten those depressing times. The 1950s saw the start of the flower clubs and a new interest in both gardening and flower arranging came into being, to the benefit of the arranger and the gardener.

There is nothing more rewarding than to see the first flower or leaf appear in the garden that you have tilled and loved. To be able to pick that flower and arrange it is the ultimate fulfilment. May this book help you do both.

PLANNING AN ARRANGER'S GARDEN

A flower arranger's garden is usually started when the gardener becomes interested in flower arranging and cannot buy the material needed to create an interesting design. From the first introduction to flower arranging, the interest grows to include not only the easily-purchased plants but also the more unusual.

Corylus avellana 'Contorta' is a flower arranger's delight.

Climbers Ivies and honeysuckles are two easy climbers that are useful for both foliage and flowers. In the garden, ivies are excellent for covering walls and fences and are sometimes used as ground cover. Although the green-leaved varieties are very shade tolerant, the variegated kinds prefer more light and are less hardy. *Hedera colchica* 'Sulphur Heart' and *H. helix* 'Goldheart' are both variegated green and gold, and established plants will reward you with a wealth of material, both for the garden and for flower arrangements.

Lonicera × americana, the creamy-white flowers of which appear in April, is a vigorous climber and is wonderfully fragrant too. Its arching branches and unusual leaf formation make it an interesting plant to use for outline material in arrangements.

Shrubs The *Salix* genus produces two unusual willows that are much loved by flower arrangers. *S. sachalinensis* 'Sekka' and *S. matsudana* 'Tortuosa' both produce branches of unusual shape, some of which are twisted and flattened. Both are fast growers that need to be kept under control. *Corylus avellana* 'Contorta' is a hazel that also produces unusual twisted branches; these are seen at their best during the winter months, before the leaves appear. Unlike the willows, this is a very slow-growing shrub.

The mahonias are hardy evergreen shrubs that flower from late winter onwards. Their yellow flowers are bell shaped and add colour to the garden. *M. aquifolium* is good as ground cover and will grow in both sun and shade.

A lovely shrub that is sometimes used as hedging and is usually grown for its foliage is the elaeagnus. The silver-leaved species prefer full sun, but *E. pungens* 'Maculata' is a large shrub with straight stems and green- and gold-variegated foliage that is ideal for use as outline material.

One of the easiest to grow of the summer-flowering shrubs is the philadelphus. Its white cup-shaped flowers are very fragrant. *P. coronareus* is known as the mock orange, but the lovely yellow-green foliage of *P.c.* 'Aureus' in early spring makes this a must in any garden.

The forsythia is one of the most popular of spring-flowering shrubs and really should be included in any

The four-petalled flower and striking thorns of *Rosa sericea pteracantha*.

garden. If you bring branches indoors before their flowering time and put them in warm water in a warm place, they can be persuaded to flower earlier than normal, giving an added bonus to the flower arranger.

An architectural plant that really looks its best when seen alone is the *Fatsia japonica*. Its very striking pollution-resistant palmate leaves are excellent for use in abstract and modern designs.

Roses Space is always difficult to find in the garden, and never more so than in the garden used for flower arrangement plant material. Although the rose is probably the most popular of all flowering shrubs, it is not always possible to grow all the varieties that you would like. But a rose that is well worth including, if only for its architectural value, is *Rosa sericea pteracantha*.

This has lovely fern-like foliage and single creamy-white flowers that bloom along the entire length of the stem in May. The flowers have just four petals, which in itself is most unusual, but the fascinating thing about this rose is its thorns. They, too, cover the length of the stem, and are very long—about 4cm (2in) at the base of the stem. When young, the thorns are a bright red, and bushes should be pruned frequently to maintain this colour. This is truly an arranger's rose.

The picker's garden Shrubs and climbers tend to produce foliage and flowers on such a large scale that an arranger would have to be very greedy to make a noticeable impact, spoiling the plant from the gardener's viewpoint. Unfortunately, when it comes to annuals and bulbs, and even some perennials, flower picking can leave a very bare and unlovely-looking patch in the border.

The ideal answer to this problem is to have a picker's garden. It is not always possible to set aside an area of the garden simply to grow flowers for picking, but if you are lucky enough to have a kitchen garden or can screen off an area of the main garden for this purpose, it is well worth considering.

With careful planning, you can grow a surprising quantity of flowers in your picker's garden, all year round. By growing flowers in orderly rows, you will be able to fit the maximum number into the space. You should also try to plan a careful progression, perhaps planting successive rows at spaced intervals, so that you do not produce a glut. If you are planting tulips, for instance, check the flowering times and buy a range of early, mid-season and late varieties.

You can also sit down and plan colours and combinations for arrangements, bearing in mind the foliage, blossom and other flowers that may be available in the main garden at the relevant times of year.

It is probably best to plant bulbs which will be picked for indoor decoration in the picker's garden, leaving the main garden with just a few to enhance the other border subjects. Tulips, daffodils and even grape hyacinths will all grow well in this way. Lilies and gladioli would also be better grown in the picker's garden, where their sudden absence will not leave an unsightly gap. Alliums, or ornamental onions, could be grown in both the main garden and the picking area.

Flower borders Of the annuals and perennials that are possibly more suitable for the main garden, *Moluccella laevis* (bells of Ireland) must be one of the most popular. A fairly fast grower, it has branching

stems and rounded leaves. The flowers are insignificant, but they are surounded by a conspicuous shell-like green calyx resembling a bell, hence the name. When mature these plants dry well, but preserving with glycerine gives a much better result.

Two unusual mid-border plants are the acanthus and the eryngium, both of which preserve beautifully. The tall stately acanthus is best seen alone, with its unusual overlapping bracts and mauve and white tubular flowers. Eryngiums are mostly blue to purple and, when dried, keep their colour very well.

Many of the *Helleborus* genus produce attractive green flowers, including *H. foetidus* and *H. lividus corsicus*. *H. niger*, the Christmas rose, has white flowers which bloom in December, hence the name, and *H. orientalis* (Lenten rose) produces its flowers in March and April. The flowers from this variety can be white, pink, purple or even maroon, for it is a very variable plant. When conditioned, they can be used in arrangements, and the foliage may

LEFT *Helleborus orientalis* is attractive in both fresh and preserved arrangements.

RIGHT Dahlias in myriad shapes and colours make a glorious display in the garden and are perfect for arranging.

BELOW The tall, distinctive flower spikes of *Digitalis* are followed by attractive seedheads.

be preserved later in the year, so some hellebores are a must in a flower arranger's garden.

Euphorbias are show stoppers in any garden. The first to appear in the border is *E. robbiae*, and what a delight the lime-green heads are, just when you thought spring would never come. You will have to be careful to keep it under control, however, as it is an invasive plant. *E. amygdaloides* 'Purpurea' is a lovely purple-leaved variety. It is sometimes susceptible to mildew, but is still worthy of a place in both the garden and flower arrangement.

E. wallachii is a fairly new variety – tall, with bright yellow heads that tend to dazzle when the sun is on them. Last but not least is *E. griffithii* 'Fireglow', with its red-orange flowers. All of these are well worth growing.

Digitalis (foxglove) varieties can be grown both for their tall stems of bell-shaped flowers and for the attractive autumn seedheads. They will thrive in most well-drained soils, as will *Alchemilla mollis* (lady's mantle). This versatile perennial will seed freely in any part of the garden. It produces small greenish-yellow flowers that are a joy to arrangers and glycerine to a beautiful light tan.

Finally, dahlias are justifiably popular, both with gardeners and arrangers. Seen at their best in bedding schemes that display their differing sizes and unusual petal formations, they are ideal for cutting and for exhibition. There are numerous varieties that are worth considering, some of which are listed in the Arranger's Selection chapter.

FOLIAGE PLANTS

The importance of foliage in flower arrangement cannot be emphasized enough. Not only does foliage enhance the flowers used in a design, but it enables the arranger to be more economical in their use. Probably the most popular of the traditional styles of design is the triangle. The outline can be of branches from one of the shrubs in the garden, such as elaeagnus or forsythia, with the visual weight toward the base. The foliage at the centre of the design might be a mixture of bergenia, ivy and arum. When combined with some flowers, the overall effect of the mixed foliages can be very pleasing and interesting.

LEFT Combining grey felted leaves with sunny yellow flowers, *Senecio* × 'Sunshine' is worthy of a place in any arranger's garden.

RIGHT The striking foliage and seedheads of *Iris foetidissima*.

Colour combinations By mixing foliages of various colours, textures and shapes, you can create an attractive design without using any flowers whatsoever. Similarly, a simple freestyle design of *Phormium tenax*, *Fatsia japonica* leaves and a lily, arranged on a pinholder in a flat dish, is not only economical with precious foliages, but easy to execute and maintain. The permutations of both flowers and foliage in a design of this type are endless.

Bergenia, hosta and arum are three of the most popular of large-leaved foliage plants grown for flower arranging. Hostas are summer-flowering perennials grown mostly for their foliage. The varied textures, shapes and colours of the leaves make hostas very rewarding, both in the garden and in arrangements. One of the good strong yellow-leaved varieties is *H.* 'Sun Power'; *H. sieboldiana* has large grey-green leaves, and *H. plantaginea* is a good plain green – just three to whet the appetite of the gardening flower arranger.

Bergenias are hardy evergreen perennials with shiny green leaves. They make good ground-cover plants, and some varieties change their leaf colour during the winter months. One of the easiest to grow is *B. cordifolia*, or elephant ears, the leaves of which can acquire attractive reddish tones in autumn and winter.

Arum leaves are arrow-head shaped, those of *A. italicum* 'Pictum' being white-veined. In addition to their use in floral designs, they provide attractive winter ground cover in the garden, and look especially striking when contrasted against one of the yellow-leaved shrubs.

It is difficult to find plants that have large red leaves, but one with purple leaves is *Heuchera* 'Palace Purple'. This has large leaves that are ideal for covering the mechanics in an arrangement. In the garden, it makes a good companion for hostas, especially the yellow varieties.

Phormium tenax has long been a favourite foliage with the flower arranging fraternity. Not only does it give a strong line to some designs, but it can also offer a contrast to the round-leaved plants in the garden. *P.t.* 'Bronze Baby' has wine-red leaves, while 'Aurora' has vertically-striped leaves of bronze, red, salmon pink and yellow. Phormiums are usually frost hardy, though some need winter protection.

Not quite as exotic as the phormium, but just as useful, is *Iris foetidissima*. This evergreen iris is welcome, both in the garden and in floral displays. Although its flowers are usually a dull purple, the seed-heads and foliage make up for this. Its sword-like leaves stand well when cut; they can be glycerined successfully and, like those of the phormiums, they offer a striking contrast of form when set against round-leaved plants.

Members of the *Plantago* genus are classed as weeds by most gardeners, but not by flower arrangers. *P. major* 'Rosularis' is a very unusual plant, having a rosette of petal-like green bracts on a medium-length stem. *P. m.* 'Atropurpurea' has bronze-purple, heavily-veined leaves, but is susceptible to mildew. It self-sows freely in the garden, if the seedheads are not removed before the seed has set.

Grey leaves Grey foliage plants are very appealing and complement a great many other colours, including pink, lilac, purple, red and blue. *Senecio* × 'Sunshine' has grey felted leaves that are useful during the winter when there is little grey foliage to pick. *S. bicolor* 'Cirrhus' has very dense grey leaves that are almost white in appearance. This is a nearly-hardy evergreen, but is usually treated as an annual.

Ballota pseudodictamnus is a sub-shrub with grey-green leaves. It is an ideal plant, both for the garden and for flower arrangements. Use it fresh during the summer and autumn, and glycerine plenty for the winter months.

The resourceful gardener would be wise to grow additional foliage plants in the picker's garden, to help supplement that which is grown in the main garden.

ALL THE YEAR ROUND

It is important to have a good range of plants in the garden, creating year-round interest and producing a continuous flow of material for flower arrangements. Spring and summer rarely present problems, for there is generally a wealth of flowers and foliages. By late summer, there may be fewer flowers for picking, but there are the delights of berries and seeds, and of beautiful foliage colours.

LEFT *Helleborus foetidus* provides cutting material in the sparse winter months.

BELOW RIGHT The pretty white berries of *Symphoricarpos albus* appear in autumn.

BELOW FAR RIGHT *Cotoneaster* berries associate well with a variegated *Ilex*.

In this context, a lovely plant to possess is *Bergenia ciliata*. This is an evergreen, though it may require protection during a very cold winter. Its leaves are round and flat, and are hairy on both sides. Green in spring and summer, they sometimes turn shades of red, orange and cream in the autumn. In the garden, this bergenia looks very attractive when planted with *Helleborus foetidus* towards the front of a border.

Hips and berries Autumn offers a rich variety of fruits for glowing designs in autumnal colours. The arum, for example, produces spikes of bright red berries that make an excellent focal point for an arrangement of autumn foliages.

During the summer, the species rose *R. glauca* has grey-purple foliage with an overlaying grey bloom, but in autumn it produces shiny red hips and the foliage changes to reds and creams. *R. moysii* has large red flask-like hips in the autumn; these attract birds to the garden and are stunning in autumn designs.

Cotoneasters, which are chiefly grown for their flowers and fruits, provide excellent outline material in autumn and early winter. *C. adpressus* has arching branches and small pink flowers, followed by spherical red berries. *C.* × 'Cornubia' is a semi-evergreen that also produces red berries, in pendent clusters.

The *Symphoricarpos* or snowberry is a delight in the autumn, when its clusters of white or pink berries appear. This hardy deciduous shrub can be planted to add colour to the shady part of the garden, and is sometimes used for hedging. Its berries, which are usually large and globose, appear during October and persist through to February. *S. albus* 'Laevigatus' has white berries and those of *S. orbiculatus* are pink. Both are a pleasure to use in designs; sprays of the white berries, for example, can be arranged with holly, ivy and red carnations for a very pretty Christmas decoration.

Evergreens After the deciduous shrubs have shed their leaves and the herbaceous plants have died down, it is time for the evergreens to play their part in helping to enhance both the home and the garden.

The most instantly recognizable of all evergreens must surely be the *Ilex*, or holly. These are generally grown for their attractive foliage and berries, but to produce berries it is necessary to grow male and female plants together. If space is at a premium in your garden, however, and you have room for only one variety, the leaf colour of many of the variegated varieties more than compensates for the lack of fruit.

The more architectural shrubs can be seen at their best now, and as many of them produce attractive leaves and, sometimes, winter flowers, space could be made for them. *Fatsia japonica* has already been recommended for its leaves and architectural value, and another shrub that is similarly rewarding is *Mahonia* × 'Charity', which is tall, with large spiny leaves and sprays of yellow scented flowers, appearing from December onwards. As the weather becomes colder, its leaves often turn a colourful range of reds, creams and orange. Elaeagnus, fatsia and mahonia, with their striking leaf shapes and bold outlines, are really year-round shrubs, but they are seen at their best during the winter months.

One of the most dominant and exciting of the winter shrubs is *Garrya elliptica*, with its dark-green leaves and long grey catkins. Preferring a south-facing wall and some sunshine, it is a very imposing sight on a dark winter's day. It also provides excellent outline material for large pedestal displays, especially when preserved.

Most of us associate *Ligustrum*, or privet, with hedging, but there are several kinds, some with attractive variegated foliage, and all grow into relatively tall shrubs, providing a wealth of straight stems. These are ideal for outline material in both summer or winter arrangements. An attractive cultivar is 'Vicaryi', which has yellow leaves that glow in winter sunshine and lighten the house when used in arrangements.

COLOUR SCHEMES

Colour is a sensation that is personal to each individual, so the suggestions given here are only ideas intended to show an approach to colour design in the garden, with flower arrangements in mind. You know which colour combinations are desirable in your home, and can plan your garden accordingly. The aim, both for the gardener and the flower arranger, is to experiment with the colours provided by nature, in order to discover attractive combinations.

LEFT A warm colour scheme with red crocosmias and nicotiana, enchantment lilies, alchemilla and penstemons.

BELOW RIGHT Cool tones in a border presided over by *Chrysanthemum serotinum.*

Warm and cool colours Reds, yellows and oranges are known as advancing, or warm, colours, while blues and greens are cool and tend to recede from the eye. For example, if you plant yellow achilleas, red crocosmias and orange day lilies, *Hemerocallis*, in a group, you will create a lively and exciting display. In an arrangement, the same effect could be achieved by using the same achilleas and crocosmias, but substituting orange dahlias for the day lilies, which do not last when picked.

If the need were for a cooler, more soothing effect, you might try eryngium, grouped with *Acanthus mollis*, and set against a background of grey-green *Garrya elliptica*. Alternatively, mix complementary colours, blending the cool with the warm. Blue *Camassia leichtlinii* might be planted alongside orange tulips, for example, or try yellow forsythia underplanted with purple crocuses.

Very attractive effects can be created, both in the garden and in flower designs, with monochromatic schemes, mingling varying tints, tones and shades of one colour. A planting of all-green foliage with the emphasis on form and texture is always pleasing. *Phlomis russelliana*, with its tall square-shaped stems and well-spaced flower heads, might be planted with *Hellerborus lividus corsicus, Paeonia laxifolius*, the pleated leaves of *Crocosmia paniculatus* and *Heuchera* 'Greenfinch', creating a quiet oasis in an otherwise colourful garden.

If you are adventurous, on the other hand, you could create a polychromatic scheme reminiscent of the Dutch and Flemish masters, planting a riotous mixture of species in as many colours as possible.

Seasonal schemes Whichever plan you finally adopt in your garden, bear in mind the uses to which the resulting plant material might be put inside the house. The following examples show how an arranger with a decor that demanded floral designs in peach and cream might be able to use home-grown materials in successive seasons.

SPRING
Style: freestyle
Outline material: *Salix sachalinensis*
Transitional material: *Fatsia japonica*
Extra interest foliage: none
Flowers: either yellow or peach gerberas, or orange double tulips, or *Dianthus* 'Valencia'

When arranging the above, pick willow branches that will give movement and interest to the design, stripping off the leaves. The fatsia leaves should be immaculate, and you will find that you can improve their sheen if you wipe them with a little oil. Don't use too many flowers—remember that space is as important as the flowers in an arrangement.

SUMMER
Style: traditional, in a raised container
Outline material: *Berberis thunbergii* 'Atropurpurea'
Transitional material: *Heuchera* 'Palace Purple'
Extra interest foliage: yellow hosta leaves and perhaps *Alchemilla mollis*
Flowers: peach roses, *Achillea* 'Great Expectations' or 'Salmon Beauty', and *Cosmos atrosanguineus*

This is more lavish with material than the spring arrangement. Remove the thorns from the base of the berberis before conditioning it. If you are using the achillea, strip the damaged and unwanted leaves from this before conditioning.

AUTUMN
Style: traditional, using preserved and fresh materials
Outline material: glycerined moluccella or ballota
Transitional material: glycerined mahonia leaves
Extra interest foliage: glycerined *Alchemilla mollis*
Flowers: dark red roses or dahlias, cream spray chrysanthemums, crocosmia seedheads

The preserved material for the autumn design is in various shades of cream and brown. Moluccella will be slightly paler than ballota, and mahonia is a light tan. A lovely dark-red rose is *R*. 'Intrigue', which would be very dramatic in this design.

A winter arrangement might use a similar blend of preserved and fresh materials, perhaps with colour from winter jasmine, with its yellow blossoms, the white flowers of *Helleborus niger*, and the white berries of *Symphoricarpos albus*.

17

AFTERCARE

The aftercare of plants is as important as the planning and planting of the garden. Pests and diseases can damage plants and affect the general appearance of your garden, and it is particularly important to keep flowers and foliage as fresh and unharmed as possible if you are intending to use them in an arrangement. Slight blemishes that pass unnoticed in the garden show up considerably more clearly in the dining table centrepiece. For this reason, it makes sense to give extra attention to plants that are intended for picking.

LEFT When other gardeners are dead-heading, the flower arranger is gathering a wealth of attractive material.

RIGHT Stake tall plants well from an early stage.

By keeping your garden neat and tidy, you will cut down on unnecessary work and at the same time lessen the number of potential breeding grounds for pests and fungal diseases. If you decide to make compost, either use a bin or make a special enclosure, but do not risk putting diseased leaves, stems or roots on the compost.

Indiscriminate dead-heading is, however, a thing to be avoided in the flower arranger's garden—indeed, some of the plants may have been grown for their seedheads and the species roses for their hips, and these must be left to ripen on the plant before being cut for use.

Feeding and mulching Mulches can play an important part in weed control, while at the same time keeping the soil moist. A mulch usually consists of a bulky organic material that is applied as a top dressing, one of the most commonly-used mulches being 'Forest Bark' Ground and Composted Bark. Make sure that the ground is thoroughly moist before you apply the material.

Once established, plants should not need watering—in theory—but this may be necessary during a prolonged dry spell and for newly-planted shrubs. Make sure that you water plants thoroughly—inadequate watering can cause roots to develop too close to the surface.

An application of a general granular fertilizer, such as Growmore, at the start of the growing season will help to produce healthy blooms. During the growing season, additional feeding with a liquid fertilizer, such as Miracle-Gro or ICI Liquid Growmore, boosts flowering plants.

Staking It may be necessary to stake some plants, so choose your stakes carefully and erect them before the plants are too large. There are many different kinds of supports available. Small twigs are quite suitable for plants such as *Alchemilla mollis*, whereas paeonies will require much stouter and taller stakes. One of the newer metal-ring types of support now available is designed so that you can add to it as the plant grows.

Pests and diseases These are disastrous from a flower arranger's viewpoint, so you must check plants regularly and deal with any problems before they take a hold. Aphids multiply at an alarming rate and not only weaken plants by sucking sap but also spread diseases. They should be destroyed as soon as possible, and regular applications of an insecticide spray such as 'Sybol' throughout the growing season will help to keep a check on infestations.

Grubs that burrow into bulbs can be kept in check with a dusting of an insecticide such as 'Sybol' Dust.

Slugs and snails are a great nuisance. Leaves may survive the odd nibble but they will not be usable for flower arrangements, and in mild, damp weather slugs and snails can thrive, causing immense destruction. Hostas are a favourite food, so protect them with a scattering of ICI Slug Pellets before a serious attack has got under way.

Fungal diseases, including rusts and mildews, can disfigure plants even when they do not destroy them. A precautionary measure is to remove any diseased leaves as and when you see them, before insects have spread the problem to other plants. Rose leaves with black spot, for example, should be taken from the plant and destroyed. If you notice signs of fungal attack, a thorough spraying with a general systemic fungicide, such as 'Nimrod'-T or Benlate + 'Activex' 2, will help to deal with the disease before it becomes a serious problem.

Slugs can devastate precious foliage.

19

GROWING UNDER GLASS

If you are fortunate enough to have a greenhouse or conservatory, you may be tempted to grow some flowers or foliage plants that you can use as cut material in your arrangements. It is economical and rewarding to be in a position to avoid the flower shops and benefit, even during the winter months, from home-grown Christmas roses, carnations, chrysanthemums and attractive foliages. It is pleasant to have flowers a little earlier than would be the case if they were grown outside, and you can also ensure that they are undamaged by wind or frost. This is also your chance to grow plants, such as *Nerine sarniensis* hybrids, that are not sufficiently hardy to be grown outdoors.

ABOVE RIGHT
Cobaea scandens is a graceful climber well worth finding room for in a greenhouse or conservatory.

LEFT
Carnations *(Dianthus)* grown under glass provide colour and a mass of material for flower arrangements throughout the year.

Greenhouse rules There are several points to remember when raising greenhouse flowers. The first is that plants will require watering far more frequently when grown under glass than when grown in the garden, particularly during the summer months. Adequate ventilation is imperative, especially during the summer, when the greenhouse is full, and also in the winter if the weather requires it. Shading is also essential; if the temperature rises over 29°C (85°F), plants may be damaged.

A GREENHOUSE SELECTION

The range of flowers that you choose to grow will depend to a large extent on the amount of space available and the other uses to which your greenhouse or conservatory is put. The following is just a selection, but many others, such as freesias or lilies, are well worth considering.

Chrysanthemums The numerous greenhouse varieties and cultivars, known as late chrysanthemums, provide flowers from October to December. The plants stand outside in their pots until the first frosts are expected, when they should be taken inside. Before taking them inside, spray for pests and diseases. You can grow single chrysanthemums as sprays by removing the crown bud from each shoot; this will produce lots of flowers during November and

December. Spider or rayonnante varieties have long quilled petals in white, yellow, pink and bronze.

Cobaea scandens A rather unusual climber for growing under glass, the cup and saucer vine is frost tender and requires a minimum temperature of 4°C (39°F). This tendril climber, with its yellow-green flowers that turn purple as they age, is an evergreen. There is also a white variety, *C. s.* 'Alba', with flowers that open green and age to white. Cut both varieties hard back when flowering has finished.

Dianthus The perpetual flowering carnations are usually unscented, with double flowers, and they are available in a large colour range. Disbud the flower stems, leaving one terminal bud per stem. Most of the Sim varieties are good, with a fine mixture of colours. 'The Joker' (crimson), 'Harvest Moon' (golden yellow) and 'Lena' (salmon pink) are just three recommended varieties. They require a temperature of 8–9°C (46–48°F) to ensure good flower production. They also require full light and adequate ventilation.

Gerbera This has a simple daisy-like flower, but with its range of colours it is a real favourite with both flower arranger and gardener. Gerberas bear a single flower on a long stem and require a minimum temperature of 7°C (45°F). Plant in John Innes No. 1, adding coarse sand for good drainage. 'Helios' is a single red flower, whereas 'Jeanette' is a double pink. 'Terra Mix' has salmon-pink petals shading to cerise pink towards the centre. Propagate either from cuttings or seed in spring, and water sparingly.

Rosa The commercial growers produce lovely roses as cut flowers all the year round, but for the amateur this is almost impossible. There is, though, one rose that is a true greenhouse variety: 'Columbian Climber' has a height and spread of 3m (10ft), and produces very fragrant, pure pink flowers of the hybrid tea type on very long stems with mid-green leaves. It is an ideal rose for both cutting and decorative value. As it is not frost hardy, it does require some heat in winter.

For an early rose, put a hybrid tea type into a 17.5cm (7in) pot in September, and take it into your greenhouse or conservatory in December, making sure that you keep the temperature above 7°C (45°F). Prune in January, and the rose will flower in April. This is very useful when there are no roses in the garden, and they are at their most expensive at the florist's.

Zantedeschia The arum lily is much favoured by all flower arrangers for its use at Easter time. Although usually grown in the flower border, it can be grown in the greenhouse or conservatory for earlier flowers. Pot in late summer in John Innes No. 1. Arum lilies require a minimum temperature of 10°C (50°F) and take approximately 13 weeks to flower.

CONDITIONING YOUR MATERIALS

Gathering and conditioning your fresh plant materials is the last vital step before you arrange them. If flowers and foliages are not well conditioned, they will not last and your arrangement will soon die.

Cut your flowers with a clean, slanting cut, and place the stems immediately into a bucket of water to stop the ends from sealing over. Make sure you have stripped off any leaves that are damaged or that will be below the level of the water.

Gathering Gather your chosen material either in the early morning or in the evening. Avoid cutting during the warmest part of the day, when the plants are losing moisture and may be wilting. Cut each stalk with a slanting cut, creating a large surface area to take up water. Take a bucket of water with you when cutting, and place the cut material directly in water. This prevents the stem ends from sealing over, and more water is readily absorbed.

Use strong sharp scissors or, if you prefer, a sharp knife to cut your material. Cutting clean helps to prevent bacteria forming and also prolongs the life of the finished arrangement. Remove any damaged leaves and those that would come below the surface of the water.

Conditioning Remove rose thorns and strip off about 5cm (2in) of the lower bark; this helps the stem to take up water. Chrysanthemum stems should be slit upwards for about 2.5cm (1in) with a sharp knife. Scrape about 5cm (2in) of bark from the base of other woody stems.

The euphorbias exude a milky sap and require a different kind of conditioning. When cutting euphorbias, keep them separate from other material. If the stem is very milky, dip it briefly into the soil before placing it in the water. When you are ready to condition them, recut and burn the stem ends with a naked flame, making sure the end is sealed, then plunge the stems into tepid water and leave for at least six hours or preferably overnight. Poppies should also be conditioned in this manner.

All plant material requires at least six hours' conditioning for you to get the best from it. Branches need to be washed, as do large leaves. Add a little washing-up liquid to the water, give the foliage a quick swish and a rinse and then stand it in water to have a good long drink.

Large leaves can be submerged for their drink, but don't over-condition them. A good method is to leave them submerged for two hours, then put them into a polythene bag and seal the end; in this way, your leaves will keep for at least a week.

This treatment does not apply to grey-leaved plants, which should never be submerged. The grey appearance is caused by thousands of small hairs covering the surface of the leaf, and if these become wet the leaves lose their grey colouring and become waterlogged. Simply stand such leaves in about 5cm (2in) of water to condition them. This also applies to any of the furry leaves, such as those of the foxglove.

Special treatments Delphiniums and lupins have hollow stems that must be filled with water. The simplest method is to use a small narrow-spouted watering can or syringe. Fill the hollow stem with water and plug the end with a piece of cotton wool or, in dire emergencies, tissue paper. Place the stem in water—the cotton wool will act as a wick and keep the stem full.

Roses, especially garden ones, sometimes develop an airlock in the stems when cut, causing the heads to droop. To counteract this, place about 5cm (2in) of water in a pan and bring it to the boil. Protect the flower heads by wrapping them in tissue or covering them with a paper bag; remove the lower leaves; recut the ends, and place the stem ends in the boiling water for 15 seconds. Remove the roses from the pan and place them in deep tepid water for at least two hours before using them.

Hellebores are notoriously difficult to condition, especially during the early part of the year. Most respond to the same treatment as the rose, but even this treatment is not always successful. They are easiest to use as a cut flower after they have set seed, when they hold their moisture content better and last longer in flower arrangements.

There are now some very good flower foods on the market. These have been manufactured with the flower arranger in mind, and recent experiments have found them to be effective in prolonging the life of cut plant material and flowers. When you use these foods, always follow the manufacturer's instructions precisely for the best results.

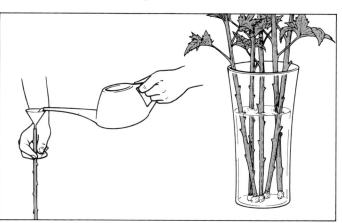

Flowers such as lupins and delphiniums must have their stems filled with water to prevent them from wilting once they are cut. Use a watering can with a narrow spout; when full, plug the stem ends with cotton wool and place them in water.

DRYING AND PRESERVING

This is one of the most fascinating aspects of flower arranging, especially if you have grown and preserved your own materials. There are three ways to preserve plant materials for arrangement: air drying, desiccants and glycerining.

OPPOSITE TOP
Single or flat leaves should be glycerined in a shallow dish.

LEFT Air drying is simple and suitable for a wide range of plant material.

OPPOSITE BOTTOM
Pour desiccant over flower heads in a plastic box, making sure the heads are not touching.

Air drying This is by far the easiest method, most of the plant material to be dried being available from middle to late summer. Cut and remove all damaged and unnecessary leaves; tie the stems in small bunches, and hang upside-down in a cool, dark but airy place. To help keep the colour, cover the flower heads with brown paper bags. Delphiniums and achillea benefit from this treatment. Helichrysum, statice, amaranthus, eryngium and moluccella all dry well by air drying, but they must be cut before reaching maturity, as they continue to develop while they dry.

Drying in desiccants Desiccants will dry plant material without loss of colour or shape. It is recommended that only individual flowers and small sprays of leaves are dried this way, and you should dry one type of flower at a time.

The desiccant extracts the moisture from the plant material, but leaves it intact. Of the desiccants that are available, silver sand, borax and silica-gel are the three most commonly used. Silver sand is easily obtained from your local garden centre; borax can be purchased from the chemist, and silica-gel is available from craft shops or, if you are a member of a flower club, from your sales table.

To dry flowers, cut the stems to within 2.5cm (1in) of the heads—the dried flowers can be wired later, ready for use. Put a 2.5cm (1in) layer of desiccant in the bottom of your drying box (plastic ice-cream tubs are useful), turn each flower gently in the desiccant, then arrange them in a single layer, not touching. Place single flowers head up, and spikes sideways. Now carefully pour desiccant over each flower. With multi-petalled flowers, such as roses, tease the petals slightly apart with a cocktail stick to make sure that there is desiccant between petals. Gently tap the box from time to time, to eliminate air pockets. Finish with a 2.5cm (1in) layer of desiccant on top. Seal the box, and store in a warm dry place.

Drying times vary greatly, and some flowers can take up to three weeks. Check after three or four days. When the flowers are finally dry, they will feel papery to the touch. Any desiccant that sticks to the leaves can be brushed away with a fine paint-brush.

The finished flowers should be kept in a large box, preferably plastic, to which has been added a small amount of the desiccant. This helps to prevent the plant material re-absorbing moisture from the atmosphere. Place a lid on the container and seal it with sticky tape.

Glycerine and antifreeze Many foliages and some seedheads can be preserved by this method, though it is not successful with many flowers. The material changes colour, the range running from cream to brown. Preserved leaves will last indefinitely and can be dusted or even wiped with a damp cloth.

Antifreeze is cheaper than glycerine and works in much the same

way, but the results are not always as good. The final colour varies according to the solution. The mixture is either one part glycerine to two parts hot water, well mixed, or equal parts antifreeze and hot water. Choose only perfect materials, removing any damaged or diseased leaves, and use a glass container. This will enable you to see when the liquid needs topping up.

On woody stems, scrape the bottom 5cm (2in) of bark away. Stand the material in the solution, which should be about 10cm (4in) deep, and place in a cool but well-lit room. Single leaves—of bergenia or fatsia, for example—are better preserved by laying them in the solution in a shallow dish.

Some materials take much longer than others. Moluccella takes only three days, but aspidistra leaves can take up to three months. When the material begins to change colour, this usually indicates that it is ready to be removed from the solution. Dry the stem ends and hang the preserved material upside-down for a few days. This helps the solution to reach the tips of the material. If you require a paler colour effect, place your finished material in the sunshine (on a window-sill) until you have achieved the desired shade.

AN ARRANGER'S SELECTION

The following is inevitably only a small sample from the vast number of plants that could justifiably have a place in the flower arranger's garden. This particular selection has been made because the plants offer a good range of colour and interest, including foliage and flowers. Many have the added benefit of fragrance, and if you choose with care from this list—adding any personal favourites that have been omitted—you will have ample material for lovely arrangements in winter and summer alike.

Antirrhinum majus 'Liberty Mixed'

SHRUBS AND CLIMBERS

Corylus avellana 'Contorta'

The corkscrew hazel is a slow-growing bushy shrub, with contorted twisted branches—an arranger's delight—and long yellow pendulous catkins. These appear during early spring, and are followed by dark-green contorted leaves. Reaching an eventual height of some 6.5m (20ft), with a spread of 5m (15ft), this large shrub prefers a well-drained soil in an open sunny site, with some protection from the east winds. It should be planted any time between October and March and can be propagated by layering in the autumn.

Elaeagnus pungens 'Maculata'

This has a height and spread of 3m (10ft) and is a lovely hardy evergreen shrub, with gold-splashed green leaves and, sometimes, spiny stems. It is an excellent garden plant, with its bright colouring, and just as excellent as a provider of foliage for decoration. *E. p.* 'Macu-lata' can be planted in April or September in ordinary soil, in sun or partial shade, and will grow in poor or chalky soils. It may be increased by cuttings taken in late August or September. No pruning is needed, but if 'all green' shoots appear they must be cut out immediately. It is prone to leaf spot, and if it shows signs of this it should be sprayed with Benlate + 'Activex' 2.

Fatsia japonica

This architectural evergreen shrub produces white flowers during autumn, followed by large black berries. Its leaves—so useful to arrangers—are a mid-to-dark green, with paler undersides, and are palmate, with seven to nine lobes. Fatsias prefer a good garden soil in a sheltered position, in sun or shade, and are tolerant of pollution, so they will thrive happily in a city garden. They can reach an eventual height and spread of some 3m (10ft), but are sometimes sold as pot plants and are also good conservatory plants. They may need some protection in the north.

Elaeagnus pungens 'Maculata'

Forsythia suspensa

The winter catkins of *Garrya elliptica*

Forsythia suspensa

Against a wall, this grows to a height and spread of 3m (10ft) or more. A deciduous rambling shrub, its drooping branches make it ideal for the traditional style of arrangement. Bright-yellow pendulous flowers are borne along the previous year's shoots. Forsythia will thrive in ordinary garden soil against a wall in any aspect. It should be planted between October and March, and will often root itself where its drooping branches touch the soil. These should be separated from the parent plant in October and transplanted to a permanent position if large enough. Cut hard back, immediately after flowering, to one or two buds of old wood.

Garrya elliptica

The silk tassel bush is an evergreen with a height and spread of 5m (15ft). It has dark-green leaves and long grey-green catkins during the winter months, and is both frost hardy and quick to grow, though it requires some protection in cold areas. The male shrub has longer catkins than the female, and the branches—either fresh or preserved—are very useful in flower arrangements. The leaves turn almost black and the catkins dark grey when preserved in glycerine.

Hedera colchica 'Sulphur Heart'

Also known as 'Paddy's Pride', this ivy grows to a height of 6–9m (20–30ft) and is a hardy evergreen with large leathery ovate leaves. These have a yellow splash in the centre and shade into pale green, with a dark-green irregular border. In common with other variegated ivies, it colours best in the summer. 'Sulphur Heart' makes a fine specimen plant and covers walls and fences with dense growth. Its large leaves are

LEFT *Ilex ×
aquifolium*
'Golden King' has
attractive leaves
and berries

RIGHT Winter-
flowering
Mahonia ×
'Charity'

useful for covering the mechanics in flower arrangements.

A typical ivy, it will thrive in any soil, and can be propagated by taking 10cm (4in) cuttings from tips of shoots in July and August. Take the cutting from runner growth if a climbing plant is required, and root it in equal parts peat and sand, ideally in a cold frame.

H. helix 'Goldheart'

Sometimes called 'Jubilee', this is a rampant evergreen hardy ivy and one of the most popular. It has a small three-to-five-pointed green leaf with a yellow centre. It grows best up a wall or old tree trunk, where it can attach itself to brick or rough bark and make rapid growth.

Ilex × aquifolium 'Golden King'

A hybrid between *I. aquifolium* and *I. perado*, this is suitable for coastal areas, being hardy and resistant to pollution. 'Golden King' has yellow-margined leaves, and although it does not produce its large red berries

in quantity, it makes an excellent specimen tree and a good hedge. If you want the berries for their decorative effect, you will have to plant the tree—surprisingly, from the name, it is female—alongside a male holly, such as 'Golden Queen'. Hollies thrive in sun or shade, though variegated forms have better colouring in a sunny position. This holly can reach a height of 6m (19ft), with a spread of 5m (16ft).

Lonicera × americana

With a potential height of 10m (30ft), this is a vigorous deciduous and very fragrant climbing honeysuckle, having red-purple buds opening to creamy-white flowers. It also has an unusual leaf formation, in which the stalked flower head nestles in the centre of a shallow oval bowl formed by two enlarged leaves, fused together. The first flowers appear in April, making this a very early-flowering honeysuckle, useful for springtime arrangements, and flowering continues to June.

Plant the honeysuckle in an ordinary well-drained humus-rich soil, where it can grow with its feet in the shade and its head in the sun. Cuttings should be taken from July to August and inserted in equal parts peat and sand in a cold frame. Take out old wood occasionally after flowering. Aphids sometimes attack young shoots and flower trusses and leave them sticky and distorted. Treat with an insecticide such as 'Rapid' or 'Sybol'.

Mahonia × 'Charity'

A large evergreen, frost-hardy shrub, this is grown for its foliage and fragrant yellow flowers, which appear in winter. The leaves consist of numerous lance-shaped spiny leaflets, dark green in colour, and the flowers are in racemes at the tips of the stems, appearing from November to February. The leaves are useful in modern designs of flower arrangements and preserve well by glycerining.

This mahonia will grow to a height and spread of 3m (10ft), and should be planted in good, preferably moist and leafy, soil, in sun or partial shade in late spring or in autumn. To propagate, take cuttings in October or November and root in equal parts peat and sand. It is best to use a propagating frame with a bottom heat of 16–18°C (61–64°F).

Philadelphus coronarius 'Aureus'

This is a hardy shrub with a dense, bushy growth, reaching a height of 2–3m (6–9ft). The young spring foliage is bright yellow; this fades to a less intense yellow green during the summer months.

Plant in any well-drained soil in shade or semi-shade between October and March. Propagation is by 10cm (4in) cuttings of half-ripe lateral shoots, taken during July and August. Insert into equal parts peat and sand in a cold frame. Hardwood cuttings can also be taken during October and November and rooted in a nursery bed, to be planted out the following year. Although generally trouble-free, *Philadelphus* does sometimes have leaf spot, which should be treated as soon as it is sighted with Benlate + 'Activex' 2.

Salix matsudana 'Tortuosa'

The dragon's claw willow is a fast-growing deciduous tree, with green bark and narrow, bright-green leaves. It can reach a height of 15m (50ft), but most flower arrangers keep it under control, plundering it for its curiously twisted branches, which are ideal in designs featuring water in spring. There is an orange-barked form which has a more spreading habit.

Plant willows between October and February in moist soil in a sunny position. It is easy to propagate both this and the following variety from hardwood cuttings taken between October and March. Insert these into moist soil in a nursery bed and plant them out into permanent positions the following year when they have become hardy enough for outdoor life.

S. sachalinensis 'Sekka'

This is a deciduous, spreading willow, which is fully hardy and is usually grown by the flower arranger for its flattened, twisted branches. It produces grey-pink catkins in late winter to early spring, followed by lance-shaped leaves of a bright, glossy green. It is a vigorous shrub that can reach a height of 5m (15ft), with a spread of 10m (30ft).

ROSES

Roses require a good rich soil with good drainage, plenty of moisture and an open sunny site. Plant any time between October and early April, in suitable weather, making sure the plants have adequate space in which to grow. The species roses will require more space than the floribundas and hybrid teas.

Rosa moyesii 'Geranium'

A species rose, this grows to a height of about 3.6m (12ft) with a spread of

Salix matsudana 'Tortuosa'

Salix sachalinensis 'Sekka'

Rosa moyesii 'Geranium' hips

3m (10ft). The flowers are single and scarlet in colour, and are followed by red hips some 5.5cm (2¼in) long.

R. rubrifolia
Another species rose, this is grown by flower arrangers for its grey-purple foliage. Plants have a height of 2m (7ft) and spread of 1.5m (5ft).

R. sericea pteracantha
Introduced from China and the Himalayas in 1890, this is a species rose, reaching a height of 3m (10ft), with a spread of 1.5m (5ft). It has small, cream-white, single flowers.

R. 'Blue Moon'
A hybrid tea rose of open habit, this reaches a height of 1m (3ft) and spread of 65cm (2¼ft), and has fragrant silvery-lilac blooms.

R. 'Brown Velvet'
This floribunda is a good rose for the flower arrranger. It has a bushy habit and an unusual, brown-tinged flower that is attractive but not very fragrant. The bush reaches a height of up to 1m (3ft).

R. 'Constance Spry'
A modern shrub rose, this has a height and spread of 2m (7ft). Rose-pink, fragrant flowers appear from June to July.

R. 'Intrigue'
A very dark-red floribunda, with glossy, green foliage, this reaches a height of some 60–75cm (2–2½ft).

R. 'Pink Pearl'
This new hybrid tea rose, with an approximate height of 1m (3ft), requires plenty of space between plants, as it spreads some 60cm (2ft). It is a strong, upright bush with disease-resistant, dark-green foliage and blush-pink flowers borne on smooth stems. It was introduced to mark the pearl anniversary of the National Association of Flower Arrangement Societies.

R. 'Shocking Blue'
A floribunda rose, this has healthy, disease-resistant foliage and very fragrant flowers, reminiscent of

Rosa 'Constance Spry'

Rosa 'Whisky Mac'

those of a hybrid tea variety. Bushes are about 75cm (2½ft) high.

R. 'Whisky Mac'
This hybrid tea rose forms a neat, upright bush, reaching a height of 75cm (2½ft), with a spread of 60cm (2ft), and bearing exquisitely-formed amber-yellow flowers.

PERENNIALS

Acanthus mollis
A semi-evergreen perennial, bear's breeches makes an excellent plant for a position towards the back of the border. It produces purple and white flower spikes to a height of 45cm (1½ft) during the summer, and the long glossy leaves are mid-green in colour and heart shaped at their base. The flower spikes can be cut when mature and either preserved with glycerine or hung in bunches and allowed to dry. Bear's breeches prefer a sunny or lightly-shaded position in deep well-drained soil and should not be disturbed until overcrowded. They should be planted between October and March. Plants reach a height of about 1m (3ft), and should be set some 60cm (2ft) apart.

Achillea
The galaxy hybrids, introduced from Germany, make a colourful corner in the garden. They last well when cut, and can be hung in a dark airy place to dry.

A. 'Appleblossom' is a mauve pink; *A.* 'Great Expectations' a sandy yellow; *A.* 'Salmon Beauty' a light salmon pink, and *A.* 'The Beacon' is a good crimson red, making a bold display when planted with *Senecio bicolor* 'Cirrhus'. Heights range from 60 to 90cm (2 to 3ft).

A. taygetea 'Moonshine' has flat-headed flowers of bright yellow set above ferny foliage of silver grey. It is an excellent cut flower and dries well for winter decorations. Its height is approximately 45cm (1½ft). All the achilleas like a sunny site with well-drained soil.

Achillea 'Great Expectations'

Alchemilla mollis

Also known as lady's mantle, this is an easy plant to grow, self-seeding freely. The yellow-green flowers and slightly hairy, palmate foliage, with its serrated edges, make an attractive addition to mixed bouquets and other arrangements. In the garden, the plants, which reach a height of about 50cm (20in), make a striking combination with clumps of purple-blue *Campanula glomerata*.

Arum italicum 'Pictum'

A frost-hardy, tuberous perennial, this is grown mainly for its bold white-veined leaves, which appear in late autumn. The leaves are borne on semi-erect stems and are arrow shaped. The green-white spathes appear in late spring and are followed by spikes of red berries, about 30cm (1ft) long, in autumn. The veined leaves are a boon for the flower arranger during the winter months, when foliage is scarce, and the spikes of red berries make good focal points in autumnal designs.

Bergenia cordifolia purpurea

Plant from midsummer to early autumn in any ordinary garden soil. *Arum italicum* should preferably be sited in the shade, but it will tolerate a sunny site. As this is not a very tall plant, it looks attractive at the front of the border, or under trees.

Ballota pseudodictamnus

This is a frost-hardy everygreen sub-shrub, which requires full sun and a well-drained soil. It has a height of 60cm (2ft) and a spread of 90cm (3ft). The flowers are inconspicuous, but the calyces surrounding them are very attractive and stems preserve well with the glycerine method. For a striking colour combination, try planting it with *Heuchera sanguinea* 'Palace Purple'.

Bergenia cordifolia purpurea

Bergenias are good hardy herbaceous perennials and make excellent ground cover. *B. c. purpurea* has rounded leaves with heart-shaped bases and bell-shaped pink-purple flowers in March and April. The attractive, useful leaves have a delic-

Arum italicum 'Pictum'

ate purple tinge to them. Plants have a height of 30cm (1ft), and they should be planted some 30–40cm (1–1¼ft) apart.

ABOVE *Cosmos atrosanguineus*
BELOW *Digitalis lutea*

Cosmos atrosanguineus
This is a chocoholic flower arranger's dream, with chocolate-scented flowers of an almost maroon-brown velvet on long thin stems. The seedheads are almost equally attractive when arranged, for example, with peach roses and copper chrysanthemums. In the garden, this cosmos makes an elegant contrast with alchemillas.

This is a half-hardy herbaceous perennial, so its tubers require lifting and storing during the winter in cold areas. Basal cuttings can be taken in the spring. *Cosmos atrosanguineus* thrives in a sunny position in a moist but well-drained soil, reaching a height of 60cm (2ft), with a spread of 45cm (1½ft).

Digitalis lutea
This bears small yellow flowers on erect stems with glossy, lance-shaped, tapering leaves with serrated margins. Plants are up to 1m (3ft) high in flower and, as with other foxgloves, the dried seedheads make a useful addition to the flower arranger's store cupboard for use as winter decoration.

Eryngium
There is something about sea hollies that appeals to both the gardener and the flower arranger. *E. giganteum* is a perennial, but it should be grown as a biennial as it dies after flowering. It has blue, heart-shaped, round-toothed leaves, tinged with ivory. The silver-blue, thistle-like

flowers measure 5cm (2in) across and appear in August to September. Plants are 1–2m (3–6ft) high, and should be set 60cm (2ft) apart.

E. planum is a very easy plant to grow. Its flower heads are much smaller than those of *E. giganteum*, and are of an eye-catching deep blue colour, appearing from July to September. Plants have a height of about 60cm (2ft).

Both these sea hollies are suitable for drying for winter use, but they should be cut before the flowers fade, to ensure that these keep their colour. They can also be preserved by glycerining, but in this case the flowers lose their colour. An ordinary well-drained soil in a sunny position is best for these plants.

Euphorbia
It is very difficult to select the best of the euphorbias – there are so many

Euphorbia griffithii 'Fireglow'

that are splendid for floral designs – but the following two are very colourful and look good, both in the border and in an arrangement. *E. amygdaloides* 'Purpurea' is a hardy semi-evergreen perennial with erect stems. Useful as ground cover, it makes rapid growth and will flourish in a poor soil in semi-shade. It has a height and spread of 60cm (2ft). It is susceptible to mildew.

E. griffithii 'Fireglow' has lance-shaped leaves that are mid-green with pale-pink midribs and its inflorescence of glorious flame-coloured bracts is borne in May to June. This euphorbia has an overall height of 60–65cm (2–2½ft), with a spread of 60cm (2ft).

Helleborus lividus corsicus
Like its relative *H. niger*, the Christ-

Eryngium planum

mas rose, this is a most welcome plant during the winter months. It has evergreen leaves and green cup-shaped flowers, which appear from March onwards, or in milder districts from late January.

Its leaves are thick and spiny, divided into three lobes, and the flowers, which appear as terminal clusters on thick stems, measure up to 5cm (2in) across. This hellebore prefers partial shade and a deep moist well-drained soil. Propagation can be from ripe seed during June-July, and plants will seed themselves quite readily. They have a height of some 60cm (2ft).

Heuchera

A hardy ground-cover plant, requiring moisture-retentive soil in semi-shade, *H. cylindrica* 'Greenfinch' is an evergreen perennial and, as its name suggests, it has green flowers. These are bell shaped, appearing on long stems above rosettes of lobed, heart-shaped leaves. Their colour alone endears this plant to the flower arranger. It also preserves well by the glycerine method.

H. 'Palace Purple' is grown more

Helleborus lividus corsicus

for its colourful leaves than its sprays of small white flowers. It, too, is a clump-forming plant, with heart-shaped purple leaves. It looks very attractive when grown with hostas, especially the yellow varieties. It has a height and spread of 45cm (1½ft).

Hosta

No garden should be without hostas. They are the flower arranger's dream and the slug's delight. The huge variety of colours, textures and sizes makes it difficult to select particular cultivars. The earliest to appear is *H. montana* 'Aurea Marginata'. This is a large plant, with leaves 30cm (1ft) wide and 35cm (1¼ft) long, very spectacular when mature. The leaves last a long time when they are cut.

A good yellow is *H.* 'Sun Power', with leaves 12.5cm (5in) wide and 25cm (10in) long. These keep their colour well until the frosts arrive.

H. sieboldiana is another large plant, with grey-blue heavily-veined leaves, but *H. plantaginea* is a plain

Hosta 'Sun Power'

Phlomis russelliana

green, and bears fragrant white flowers in August. Again heavily-veined, the leaves are almost round, being 17.5cm (7in) wide and long.

Hostas require a rich well-drained but moist soil, and most prefer shade, although there are some exceptions. They should be planted from October to March, when the weather is suitable, and they need protection from slugs and snails.

Phlomis russelliana
This unusual herbaceous perennial can be well used both in its fresh state and preserved. It has large, wrinkled basal leaves, mid-green in colour, and yellow, two-lipped flowers, arranged in whorls along the length of its square-shaped stem. After the flowers have finished, the seedheads can be preserved by glycerining, when they turn a dark brown. Phlomis prefer ordinary soil in a sunny position and should be planted from October to April, or you can sow seed in April in a cold frame. They have a height of 90cm (3ft), with a spread of 1.2m (4ft).

Plantago major
Plantains are classed as weeds by most gardeners, but the two listed here are very useful in arrangements. *Plantago major* 'Rosularis' is a herbaceous perennial with heavily-veined, long-stalked green leaves. Its flower spike is reduced to a dense rosette of petal-like green bracts, which strongly resemble a rose in formation. It looks very attractive in an arrangement of mixed foliage.

P.m. 'Atropurpurea' has bronze-purple, veined leaves, useful for covering the mechanics in a flower arrangement, and a flower spike of a similar shade.

Both these plantains are self seeding and grow in well-drained garden soil in a sunny site. Sow seed when ripe or in spring. Both plants are susceptible to mildew.

ANNUALS AND BIENNIALS

Amaranthus caudatus
A half-hardy annual, this is grown for its drooping panicles of tiny red or green flowers. It lasts well in

Plantago major 'Rosularis'

water and keeps its colour when dried for winter decoration. Sow seed outdoors in late spring, and grow in rich fertile soil in sun. The plants, which are sometimes prone to attacks by aphids, reach a height of 1.2m (4ft), with a spread of 45cm (1½ft).

Antirrhinum majus

An erect perennial grown as an annual, the snapdragon flowers from spring to autumn. There are many excellent named varieties, with a wide range of colours and sizes. All prefer full sun and a well-drained soil. They are best grown from seed, sown in pots or in pans in February or March at a temperature of 16-18°C (61-64°F).

Delphinium consolida

Larkspur can be used fresh or dried. This lovely annual, up to 1.2m (4ft) high, has mid-green leaves cut into several linear segments, giving it a ferny appearance. Long racemes of blue, pink, red, purple or white flowers open from June to August.

Seeds should be sown in spring, or autumn in milder areas. Young plants need protection from slugs and snails, and the tall stem will require support.

Digitalis purpurea

An upright short-lived perennial, but grown as a biennial, this produces 1–1.5m (3–5ft) spikes of spotted flowers in purple, red or maroon, appearing in midsummer.

Seed should be sown outdoors in May or June, and the seedlings transplanted to their flowering position in September, in ordinary garden soil in partial shade, so that they do not dry out in the summer. The whole plant should be cut down in October. Foxgloves are good for height in large displays. When the

flowers have finished and before the seeds have ripened, the stems may be dried or preserved in glycerine.

Euphorbia marginata

This is a half-hardy, bushy, fast-growing upright annual, having bright-green leaves with white margins. It grows in ordinary garden soil in sun or partial shade. Sow seed in the flowering site in March or April.

Helichrysum bracteatum

Helichrysums produce papery, daisy-like flowers from summer to early autumn, in many colours, ranging through red, pink, orange and yellow to white. This half-hardy annual grows to a height of 1m (3ft) and thrives in a well-drained soil in full sun. For drying, the flowers should be cut before their central disc is showing. Strip away unwanted leaves and hang in bunches to dry.

Limonium sinuatum

This is a slow-growing, bushy, half-hardy perennial, but it is grown as an annual. It will thrive in an

Amaranthus caudatus

40

Limonium sinuatum

ordinary well-drained soil in an open sunny site. Its clustered flowers are small and tubular, in a range of colours including pink, yellow and blue, and appear in summer and early autumn. Plants grow to 45cm (1½ft), with a spread of 30cm (1ft).

Moluccella laevis
The flowers are insignificant but are surrounded by a conspicuous shell-like green calyx, resembling a bell, hence the common name—bells of Ireland. Plants dry well when mature, but glycerine gives better results.

A half-hardy annual, it is best started off under glass. Plant out in spring when all danger of frost is past. *Moluccella* prefers a light rich soil in an open sunny site. Plants have a height of 60cm (2ft), with a spread of 20cm (8in), and may need staking.

Nicotiana alata 'Lime Green'
This upright perennial is usually grown as an annual. It is half hardy and bears racemes of open trumpet-shaped flowers that are greenish yellow in colour, and very fragrant

in the evening. Seed should be sown under glass at a temperature of 18°C (64°F) during February or March. *Nicotiana* thrives in a rich well-drained soil and a warm sunny site. Young plants may become infested with aphids.

Nigella damascena
Commonly known as a love-in-a-mist, this is a fast-growing upright annual with feathery bright-green leaves and blue or white flowers, produced during July and August. It prefers a sunny position in a well-cultivated soil, growing to a height of 60cm (2ft). Seeds are usually sown in the flowering site during March. When the flowers have faded, the seedheads may be cut and hung upside-down to dry. Plants reach a height of 60cm (2ft).

Senecio bicolor
Senecio bicolor 'Cirrhus' and *S.b.* 'Silver Dust' are both almost hardy evergreen sub-shrubs that are treated as annuals, because they do not survive very hard winters. They have dense grey foliage with deeply-lobed leaves, that can be used to

Nigella damascena, white form

41

enhance arrangements of pinks and mauves.

They have a height of about 60cm (2ft) and can be grown in ordinary garden soil in a sunny position. In the garden, they are a good complement to larkspur.

Zinnia

Zinnias are half-hardy annuals, with dahlia-like flower heads. *Z. elegans* is a large species, growing to a height of 60–75cm (2–2½ft). Coarse upright stems carry showy purple flowers 5cm (2in) across. There are many *Zinnia elegans* hybrids now available in attractive colours. *Z. e.* 'Envy' is a green variety, much admired by flower arrangers.

Zinnias are happiest in a well-drained fertile soil in a sunny position. Propagate them by seed sown under glass in early spring.

BULBS

Allium

This genus includes many ornamental onions that are of interest to flower arrangers and gardeners.

They are hardy bulbous plants, easy to grow in a sunny, well-drained position. Smaller types look attractive in a rockery, while the larger are ideal for the herbaceous border. Large plants may need staking.

A. giganteum is a summer-flowering bulb that reaches a height of 2m (6ft) with a spread of 30–35cm (1–1¼ft). The dense, spherical umbel can grow to 12cm (5in) across, having 50 or more star-shaped purple flowers.

A. caeruleum is a clump-forming, summer-flowering, frost-hardy bulb. The flowers are blue and star shaped. It is smaller than *giganteum*, being only about 60cm (2ft) high, with a spread of 10–15cm (4–6in). The flowers can be used fresh, or, after flowering and before seeds ripen, either hung to dry or glycerined for use in winter arrangements.

Camassia leichtlinii

A hardy garden perennial bulb, this grows best in a heavy moist soil that does not dry out during spring and early summer. Bulbs should be left until they become overcrowded before dividing. The tall, leafless

Allium giganteum

Crocosmia × crocosmiiflora 'Citronella'

The distinctive blooms of *Dahlia* 'Pink Giraffe'

stem bears a dense spike of star-shaped, white or bluish-violet flowers. *C. l.* 'Semiplena' has double cream-white flowers. Both grow to a height of 1–1.5m (3–5ft), with a spread of 20–30cm (8–12in).

Crocosmia

These are of threefold value—their textured leaves preserve well, as do their seedheads, and the flowers are useful for cutting. Among the many available species and varieties, *C.* × *crocosmiiflora* 'Lucifer' has sword-shaped leaves and rich-red flowers on branching spikes. It grows to a height of about 1m (3ft) and can light up a dark corner of the garden. 'Citronella', which is about 60cm (2ft) high, has grey-green leaves and golden-yellow flowers.

C. masonorum has reddish-orange flowers and can reach a height of about 1m (3ft).

Crocosmias prefer a well-drained, sandy soil, with plenty of water during the summer months.

Dahlia

These tuberous perennials flower from late June until the first frosts. They are excellent for cutting and useful and decorative as bedding plants. Being half-hardy, they require lifting in autumn. Store in a frost-proof place during winter. Dahlias thrive in a sunny position in a well-drained soil. The following is just a very small selection of the many that are suitable for the flower-arranging gardener: *D.* 'Yellow Hammer', yellow single, summer-autumn flowering, height and spread 30–45cm (1–1½ft); *D.* 'Comet', dark-red, anemone-centred, height and spread 1.2m (4ft); *D.* 'Easter Sunday', white collerette flowers, height and spread 1m (3ft); *D.* 'Vicky Crutchfield', pink water-lily flowers, height and spread 1m (3ft); *D.* 'Rhonda', pale white-lilac pompon type, height and spread 1m (3ft); *D.* 'Cherida', bronze-lilac, ball-flowered, height and spread 1m (3ft), and *D.* 'Giraffe', a miscellaneous group of dahlias, orchid-like, bronze-yellow or pink barred flowers, height and spread 75cm (2½ft).

Gladiolus

This is a summer-flowering genus that has numerous attractive hybrids, available in a wide range of colours. 'The Bride' is a popular example, having white flowers with green-marked throats. One of the larger cultivars, and popular with flower arrangers, is 'Green Woodpecker'. This has green flowers with wine-red throats and it grows to a height of 1.5m (5ft), making it a good flower for pedestal arrangements. All gladioli, however, are excellent for cutting and arranging. In the garden, they show to their best advantage when planted in groups of a single colour.

Hyacinthoides hispanica

The Spanish bluebell is a spring-flowering hardy bulb, growing to a height of 30cm (1ft), with a spread of 10–15cm (4–6in). It has glossy strap-shaped leaves, and spikes of the familiar bell-shaped flowers. As with other bluebells, the seedheads, when glycerined, turn a delightful cream colour.

Lilium

Lilies are mainly summer-flowering bulbs, with colourful flowers that are often fragrant. They need to be grown in sun in a well-drained soil,

ABOVE
Gladiolus 'Green Woodpecker'

ABOVE RIGHT
Lilium
'Enchantment'

LEFT *Lilium candidum*

RIGHT *Muscari armeniacum*

and should be watered freely during the growing season.

L. candidum, the madonna lily, is a summer-flowering species with broadly funnel-shaped white flowers. It prefers a lime-rich soil and the bulb should be planted with its nose just below the surface. These classically beautiful lilies reach a height of about 1.5m (5ft).

There are many attractive hybrids

that are a delight for both gardeners and flower arrangers, and the following is only a very limited selection. *L.* 'Sterling Star' is another white summer-flowering lily, reaching a height of 1–1.2m (3–4ft). Its upward-facing cup-shaped flowers have small brown spots inside. *L.* 'Enchantment' is an old favourite; it is marvellous both for cutting and border display. Flowering in early summer, it reaches a height of 1m (3ft), and has upward-facing, cup-shaped, orange-red flowers with black-spotted throats. *L.* 'Journey's End' flowers in late summer. The flowers are a deep pink, with maroon spots, the curved petals being outward-facing and bowl-shaped. This is a large lily, growing to a height of 2m (6ft).

Muscari armeniacum
Grape hyacinths are not normally associated with flower arrangers, but the flowers last well, both in the garden and when cut. This species is a spring-flowering bulb, with small

Nerine 'Brian Doe'

fragrant deep bluebell-shaped flowers that have constricted mouths and what appear to be white 'teeth'. The bulbs will thrive in full sun in any ordinary well-drained soil. The clumps of bulbs can become congested and should be lifted and divided every three years. Seedheads glycerine well to a lovely cream colour. The flowering plants have a height of 20–30cm (8–12in).

Nerine

The nerine has long been a florist's flower, but is now increasingly being grown in the border as an autumn-flowering bulb. *N.* 'Brian Doe' is salmon pink, with strap-shaped semi-erect leaves. The lovely pale-pink flowers of *N.* 'Orion' have wavy-margined petals and recurved tips and stand out when planted with *Senecio* × 'Sunshine'. The bulbs are only moderately hardy and should ideally be planted in a well-drained soil against a sunny wall.

Tulipa

Flower arrangers love the more unusual tulip flowers, and *T.* 'Artist' falls into this category. The large flower heads are supported on 45cm (18in) stalks and are deep salmon pink and green inside, and salmon pink, purple and green outside. Planted with blue forget-me-nots, they look lovely. *T.* 'Spring Green' is another pretty tulip, similar to 'Artist', but the flowers are white, feathered with green.

The parrot tulips have frilled or fringed and sometimes twisted petals, making interesting displays as garden plants and as cut flowers. They, too, are large and come into flower late in spring.

Like most gardeners, flower arrangers love a black tulip, and the nearest you can get to black is *T.* 'Queen of the Night'. This is another later-flowering tulip, with long-lasting, dark-maroon flowers. It makes a useful bedding plant and an ideal flower for arrangers, creating a strong impact.

Plant all tulip bulbs in November, at a depth of not more than 15cm (6in), and 10–15cm (4–6in) apart, in a well-drained soil, sheltered from strong winds.

Tulipa 'Spring Green'

46

RIGHT
*Cortaderia
selloana* 'Gold
Band'

BELOW *Lagurus
ovatus*

GRASSES

Cortaderia selloana

Pampas grass is one of the largest of the grasses, up to 1.5m (5ft) tall, with sharp, outward-curving leaves. The plume-like silver panicles appear in late summer and make excellent outline material for large

arrangements. The stems dry well when cut before they reach maturity and hung upside-down in a dry, airy place. 'Silver Comet' is a useful variety, with silver-striped leaves; 'Gold Band' has yellow stripes. Plant in a sunny, sheltered site.

Hordeum jubatum

Commonly known as squirrel-tail grass, this is a short-lived tufted perennial grass, usually treated as an annual. Its feathery plumes, borne in summer and autumn, make an attractive contrast to brightly-coloured flowers in the garden and are a boon to flower arrangers.

Lagurus ovatus

Hare's-tail grass is a tuft-forming grass that has long narrow flat leaves and soft white egg-shaped panicles of flowers, borne on gold stems. This annual grass is grown from seed sown in spring and prefers a sunny, well-drained site.

INDEX AND ACKNOWLEDGEMENTS

Page numbers in **bold type** indicate illustrations

Picture credits

Gillian Beckett: 28(br), 36(t), 37(tr).
Derek Gould: 33(tl), 37(bl), 39(tl), 40, 47(t).
S & O Mathews: 4-5, 7, 18, 20, 24, 29, 33(br), 38(tr), 41(br).
Tania Midgley: 9.
Harry Smith Horticultural Collection: 8, 11(cl), 14, 15(tl,tr), 16, 17, 28(bl), 30, 31, 32(bl), 34 (tl,br), 35(bl), 36(cr), 39(br), 41(tl), 42(bl), 44(cr,b), 45(cl), 46(tl), 47(bl).
Michael Warren: 1, 6, 10, 11(tr), 12, 13, 19(tl,br), 21, 26-27, 32(br), 35(tr), 38(bl), 42(br), 43, 45(b), 46(br).

Artwork by Simon Roulstone